Dental Marketing Fusion

51 Ways to Combine Traditional Marketing with
Powerful Online Systems to
Grow Your Dental Practice

By: Mike Saunders, MBA

LEGAL NOTICES

"Claim Your <u>FREE</u> Marketing Audit That Uncovers Marketing Assets Currently Within Your Dental Practice That Are Not Being Maximized And Easily Increase Your Sales By 25% - 50% In 90 Days or Less Without Spending More Money On Advertising!"
($497 Value)

Details revealed below...

Mike Saunders, MBA author and dynamic marketing consultant, is offering an **<u>FREE</u>** incredible opportunity for you to improve your current marketing and sales systems without spending more money on advertising. Claim your free marketing audit today and discover:

- How to **quickly increase your sales by 25% - 50% in the next 90 days** without spending more money on advertising!

- How to **guarantee that your business stands head and shoulders above the competition**, so prospects will be proud and excited to buy from you.

- The **"Hidden Goldmine"** in your business and how you can capitalize on it and make big profits.

Claim Your FREE Marketing Audit and read our Dental Social Media Case Study...

www.DentalMarketingFusion.com

3

TABLE OF CONTENTS

PART ONE:
The Basics: What You Need To Know To Maximize These 51 Marketing Strategies

PART TWO:
Business Strategies To Generate
More Sales and Increase Profits

PART THREE:
Online & Internet Strategies That Generate Tons Of Prospects And Patients

PART FOUR:
Publicity Strategies That Generate
Huge Profits At Little To No Cost

PART FIVE:
Paid Advertising Strategies With Potential
For Great Returns On Your Investment

INTRODUCTION

I f you have been in business for longer than two minutes, I'm sure that you have already stumbled across something that completely surprised you and instantly opened your eyes to a world of new possibilities. Maybe it was a brand new salesperson you just hired who went on to break every sales record in your company within their first six months. Maybe it was a vendor who sold you products at prices so ridiculously cheap that it allowed you to sell the product at bargain prices and still allowed you to actually make a few bucks. Well, no matter what the event was that opened your mind to new and exciting possibilities, the fact is that you were shown indisputable proof that more success and profits were possible than you had previously believed was possible.

This book that you hold in your hands is more of that indisputable proof. So, if you are willing to read this book with pen and paper in hand, while keeping an open mind, then a business-changing revelation is exactly what you will experience today. Not only will you will find yourself believing in your business again, but you will reawaken the excitement and joy you felt years ago when you first realized that having your own business could provide you with the freedom to create your own life and future.

Now, I realize that I am making a big claim, but as you turn the pages of this book, you will see for yourself that these proven success strategies really can increase your profits. In fact, the strategies in this book are quietly being used by successful businesses all over the nation to make them large fortunes, and by applying them to your Dental Practice, you will succeed as well.

The real tragedy is that most Dental Practices are too stuck in their old and unprofitable ways to embrace the changes in the marketplace that lead to real profits.

However, I don't want to sugarcoat the reality of what will be required for you to reach a much higher level of success. ALL of the strategies in this book will require you to make changes in your business. In fact, you should only be reading this book because you are ready to implement new but proven strategies to reach your desired level of success and profit in your business. But first, let me give you a piece of golden advice. In order to implement the strategies in this book, you must to let go of every belief that doesn't directly contribute to you depositing more profits in your bank account. That is why the first chapter of my book is geared towards preparing your mindset to make more money. So, without further adieu, let's get started on growing your profits.

PART ONE:

The Basics: What You Need To Know To Maximize These 51 Marketing Strategies

CHAPTER 1

Get Your Head in the Game

Preparing your mind for success is the first step on the path to extreme success in your business during this new economy. In fact, I'll even go a step further and predict that unless you address your mindset first, you won't even implement a single one of the proven strategies in this book.

Think it sounds a bit harsh? Well, would you rather me sugarcoat it and skim over the meat and potatoes or would you rather sit down and get a seven course meal that will have you bursting at the seams with ready-to-buy, patients and profits?

See, the truth is, no matter how great the strategies are that I reveal within the pages of this book, you will never see one extra penny of profit, unless you are willing, ready and able to make the changes required. And that, my friend, requires guts, boldness and the ability to move rapidly to follow the money in your local market.

Now, let's look at how badly things turn out when Dental Practices have a stubborn and poor mindset. Several years ago there were several super-high end furniture stores within miles of each other in New England. These retailers were priced so high, that only two percent of the population in the entire nation could afford their furniture. As the economy turned, those retailers simply refused to change their business model to reflect the change in the economy. Therefore, within six short months ALL but one of those retailers went out of business.

Unfortunately, the stubborn and poor mindset also affected many other businesses who could have easily weathered the storm of this economy with just a few simple changes to their businesses. However, they chose to ignore the changing marketplace and consequently went out of business.

So, now that you know how powerful a mind-set change is to your success, let's look at four powerful keys and realities that you must embrace in this new economy:

1. **Accept that there's still money in your local marketplace.** Don't feed me that garbage that people in your area aren't buying the type of products or services that you offer. Yes, they are. There are dozens of businesses who are making unbelievable profits during this recession. The real question is, "Will yours be one of the businesses that will make the necessary changes in order to cash in during this economic downturn?"

2. **Take advantage of the opportunities that recessions create.** Every recession creates an opportunity for someone to profit. In the example of the furniture store chain that I mentioned earlier, consumers want furniture that can be delivered quickly. Ultimately, the key to your success will be determined by your ability to listen to your market. Then, all you have to do is create a product or service to meet that need and you'll instantly have increased profits.

3. **Make decisions based on facts, not news headlines.** If you're listening to talk radio, news reports and any other media source that's pumping fear, doom and gloom into your head, then turn it off right now! The majority of news media sources are in the business of

selling fear, not hope. Your focus should be on finding what your target market wants and then giving it to them at a great value. That's it. Don't let the media drive you out of business, by slowly draining away your will to fight.

4. **Change your business or go out of business.** I see so many Dental Practices who simply refuse to do things differently, but yet, they expect different results. That's the textbook definition of insanity. You must be willing to change your staff, advertising, marketing, product and/or management, and any and everything else, in order to survive during this new economy. That's the truth, plain and simple.

CHAPTER 2

The Four Keys to Creating A Marketing Plan To Explode Your Dental Practice.

W hile preparing your mindset to go to the next level in your business is the first step towards transforming your business into a marketing machine, there are several other key principles which will also impact your success. These four key factors are so important to your business success in this new economy, that unless you build your marketing strategies using them, you will have a 99% chance of failing. So, take your time with these four cornerstone principles and then implement them into your business.

Key #1: Calculate The Lifetime Value of Your Patients.

When Dental Practices hire me to help turn their business into a money-maker, one of the first things I do is calculate the lifetime value of their patients. The lifetime value (LTV) of a customer is the amount of profit each customer brings to your business over the course of their buying lifetime with your business. Now, I will show you a simple way to calculate the LTV, but unless you keep great records you should probably hire a bookkeeper to dig through receipts and calculate the numbers for you.

In order to help you calculate your lifetime customer value, I will give you an example below.

Total Amount of Patients for the year	100
Average # of purchases per customer	2
Average Purchase Amount	$125.00
(100 x 2 x $125) **Total Revenue**	**$25,000.00**
Cost to produce each product or service (including parts & labor)	$35.00
Total cost to produce product for the 100 patients *(100 x $35)*	$3,500.00
Marketing Costs for the year	$5,000.00
Total Costs	**$8,500.00**
Total Revenue - Costs = Gross Profit *($25,000 - $8,500)*	**$16,500.00**
Gross Profit	$16,500.00
Customer Lifetime Value For The Year *($16,500 / 100 patients)*	**$165.00**
So, in this example on average each patient represents $165 worth of profit.	

So, in the example I used above, on average they represent at least $165 in profit. However, it doesn't have to stop there. In fact, your goal should be to increase the lifetime value of each patient by getting them back into your business to purchase from you more often.

The reason why the lifetime value of a customer is so important is because it gives you an idea of how much you should invest in marketing to get the customer in the first place. So, in the example above the business owner knows that if he

17

spends another $5,000 in marketing in the same ways he's investing in marketing now, he can reasonably expect to double his profits. For a Dental Practice, without knowing the lifetime value of his patients, he wouldn't have the confidence to make that kind of investment in marketing.

Key #2: Find Out the Source Of Every Lead That Comes Into Your Business

If there was one piece of advice that I would want you to remember from this entire book, it would be tracking where every lead comes from that you get into your business. In order to track where your leads come from, you can ask prospects when they walk into your business or you can use special phone numbers with unique extensions in your ads. You can also use five page websites designed for a specific sale, coupons, tracking codes or anything else you can think of know exactly where your prospects are coming from.

At the end of the day, you absolutely need to know exactly where your leads are coming from, so that you can know exactly what's working in your business. Once you know where your leads are coming from, then you can begin to invest marketing in those specific areas that are generating the best leads and patients. Without tracking your leads, you will always be wasting thousands of dollars on ineffective marketing strategies.

Key #3: Calculate Your Return On Investment For Any Marketing That You Do

This crucial key builds on the previous key that I mentioned. Quite honestly, the only way to truly know your return on investment is to track the results of every marketing strategy. Once you know how much you are spending, then you will know exactly how much each marketing dollar is bringing back to your business.

For example, if you spent $500 on an ad in a local newspaper which generated two patients, who then spent a total of $3,500 in your business, your return on your investment is 700%! So for every $1 you spent, you received $7 back. That's a very good investment by my standards.

Key #4: Create Ads And Marketing Materials That Consistently Put Money In Your Pocket:

If you ever want to see a huge waste of money, then watch the ads being played during the Super Bowl. Those ads that run during the Super Bowl ads are designed to be funny and cute and win advertising awards. However, those ads rarely make their companies any real profit. As a matter of fact, those commercials are the laughing stock of the marketing industry because companies blissfully line up and pay millions for those types of "funny" ads while receiving little to no results for their marketing dollars.

The fact of the matter is, you either need to know how to write and design good ads or have the resources to hire a good copywriter. Regardless of which option you choose, I encourage you to study good copywriters so that they have a feel for what usually works. As the owner, you should definitely know how to create ads, letters and emails that generate leads. A good expert to study to learn copywriting is Dan Kennedy. Simply type in his name in Google.com and you will find tons of resources about copywriting.

Here's a quick tip sheet on the basics which every ad you create should have:

1. Use headlines that attract patients.
2. Always have a compelling offer.
3. Use a specific start date and deadline in your ad.

4. Insert testimonials from past patients.
5. Include a guarantee on your products and services.
6. Your ad must look unique and stand out from your competitors.
7. Your ad must ONLY focus on what your customer wants.
8. Have only one goal for each ad, which is to get patients to visit your business.
9. Tell the reason why you're offering the sale.
10. Write ads that are straight to the point and easy to understand.

Now, the keys to success listed above may seem like a lot of hard work, but you only have to do the hardest work in the beginning. However, the most important factor which will contribute to your success in your business is your willingness to actually implement these strategies on a consistent basis.

CHAPTER 3

Business 101: You Must Constantly Advertise Your Dental Practice...Duh!

Sounds obvious, doesn't it? But, you wouldn't believe how many Dental Practices I see who refuse to do any type of consistent marketing or advertising! That is unbelievable to me; however it is normal for many businesses. Sure, they will do a small little ad in the local newspaper once or twice a year, but that can hardly be considered marketing consistently.

If I were to ask you what kind of business you're in, what would you say? If you're like most Dental Practices that hire me, you would probably just pick a product or service that you sell and simply tell me that you are in that industry. Right? Well, I'm here to tell you that your answer to the question of what business you're in, *should* be, "I'm in the marketing business." If that was not your answer, then I already know that you're most likely having huge profit problems in your business. Many Dental Practices are in confused about what business they are in. The simplest way to look at your business is to realize that the two most important activities in your business is marketing and actually providing the dental care that you're marketing. Every day that the doors of your business is open, is a day that you should be focusing on marketing.

Over the years, I've come to the realization that most Dental Practices are not to blame for not being able to put together effective marketing campaigns. Think about when you first started your business; did you receive an instruction manual about how to get patients? Was there a course offered

21

down at the local college designed to teach you how to attract quality buying patients? Heck, no. You just went out there and told everyone what you're doing now and then you probably sat back and waited for patients to come into your business. Back then things were pretty simple and easy. However, that gravy train didn't last, did it?

Next, you probably turned to the industry publications, magazines and newsletters, which focus on products and customer service as the solution to your problems. So, over time you looked around at what the competition was doing and you probably began to think that if you also offered product or service at a lower price, patients would flock to your business too. But, is that what happened?

Maybe at first you saw a rush of patients the first time you ran a new ad or promotion with the product at a low price, but did it continue on like that? No. Then, as time went on you probably began doing less and less advertising because you weren't seeing the results from you advertising dollars. But deep down inside, you knew that you had to do some type of marketing and advertising, but you had no idea what to do. After all you're a business owner, not a marketing and advertising guy.

That is where you're terribly mistaken. See, if you want to be a *successful and profitable* business owner, you MUST become a marketing and advertising guy! Your number one job every single day is getting more patients into your business. That's it. Why, you ask? Because the only way you make money is if prospects come into your business and are willing, ready and able to pay you money in exchange for your product or service.

You don't get paid to counsel employees, do payroll and you sure as heck don't get paid to sit around all day waiting for someone to walk in. You only get paid if and when a patient pays you. So, your number one job every day when you wake up has to be getting more paying patients through your doors. The only way to do that is to become a marketing and advertising fanatic.

When you begin to look at yourself as the marketer of your business, instead of just a business owner, it will become very easy to see if you're doing the right things to attract patients or not.

In fact, every day you that you seriously want to make money, you should be running a different promotion, ad or marketing campaign. Don't tell me that patients get tired of seeing your ads, because I'm going to tell you to advertise in a different area that hasn't seen that specific advertisement or promotion yet. Don't tell me that it's too expensive, because I know about one hundred ways to advertise your business on a shoe-string budget and most of them cost less than what you spend on lunch for the week.

In order to succeed in this new economy, you MUST view yourself as the marketer of your business and NOT just an owner of a business.

CHAPTER 4

When Everybody Is Your Customer, Then Nobody Is Your Customer

One of the biggest challenges Dental Practices must overcome in order to be successful in this new economy, is the dreaded "I-offer-everything-for-everyone" syndrome. On the surface this seems like a sure-fire way to get more patients, but it's been proven time and time again that it's not always the most successful way to prosper for of 99.9%. Let's examine it closer.

There is a common slogan in marketing that states, "There are riches in niches." Simply put, this slogan means you need to determine who your most profitable, enjoyable and easy to attract customer is, and then specialize in getting more of those patients to come into your business and buy. The best way to do this is to create a U.S.P. (Unique Selling Proposition) that compels your most profitable customer to come back into your business again and again. In other words, a U.S.P. is the thing that you're known for.

The first step in developing a U.S.P. is to determine the profile of your most profitable customer. You will want to know things like; how they found your business, where they live, what newspapers and magazines they read etc.

Here's an example of some of the information that you may discover about your prospects and patients:

- Wives initially visited your business without their husbands.

24

- Recently married
- Had three kids
- Needed braces
- Got their teeth whitened
- Lived within five miles of your business
- Spent between $800 - $1500
- Paid by Visa, MasterCard or Discover

Once you have this information, you can redesign your business to cater to more of the same types of patients that are currently spending money in your business.

However, you can only use this information to your advantage if you take the time to collect it in the first place. Then you can dig deep and find out who your customer is, what's important to them and what they truly want.

CHAPTER 5

Create a 12-Month Marketing Plan...Right Now!

There is an timeless saying that goes like this: "Failing to plan means you are planning to fail." That saying is twice as true when it comes to running a business. See, some Dental Practices will not be able to weather this economic storm simply because they don't have the foggiest clue about what promotions or ads they are going to running in the next week, much less in the next month or year! However, this must change if you are going to survive and thrive in this new economy.

Now, coming up with a twelve month marketing plan may seem like a daunting task, but a benefit you receive from creating a yearly marketing calendar is you will gain a feeling of confidence and reassurance because you are not just sitting on your hands, day-in and day-out, waiting for patients to just walk in.

Let's look at a sample twelve month marketing calendar that you could create around monthly holidays:

- January – New Year's
- February – Valentine's Day
- March – President's Day
- April – April Fool's/Easter
- May – Mother's Day

26

- June – Father's Day
- July – Fourth of July
- August – (There are no major U.S. Holidays, so do a friends and family sale)
- September – Labor Day
- October – Halloween
- November – Thanksgiving
- December - Christmas

CHAPTER 6

How to Quickly Boost Your Profits by Bringing In The Big Guns

I f your son, daughter or spouse were involved in a car accident and needed specialized attention from a specific type of doctor, would you attempt to perform the surgery yourself in your garage at home? Of course not. It sounds ridiculous to even suggest such a thing, doesn't it? Well, that's how ridiculous it sounds when I hear Dental Practices, who have never even created one single successful advertisement in their twenty years in business and tell me that they refuse to hire marketing consultants.

The sad reality is most Dental Practices know they have major problems with closing ratios, marketing, sales scripts and getting patients into their business. However, they refuse to invest the necessary money to bring in experts to fix their problems.

I have come to the conclusion that failure to get expert advice is mostly due to having too much pride to ask for help or they have never even considered hiring experts in the first place.

If you really want fast results without wasting money trying out different strategies, then hiring a expert marketing consultant to help you generate more quality buying patients and convert more leads into sales, should be the first thing you do after preparing your mindset for success. Until you hire an expert consultant, you have no idea the numerous benefits your business will gain by having an expert work with you one-on-one.

With an expert marketing consultant in your business, you will no longer feel alone and isolated from other successful Dental Practices. You will no longer feel the doom and dread of having the weight of your business solely on your shoulders. Most importantly, you will have a support system to give you powerful and proven creative ideas to increase your profits.

Now, when I say expert marketing consultant, I'm not referring to some high-priced advertising agency that has no proven track record of increasing sales and profits for small to medium businesses. I am also not talking about the yellow page ad reps, radio ad reps or any other type of advertising representative trying to sell you something. I'm talking about a marketing expert who comes into your office, analyzes your business with a fine-tooth comb and then creates custom marketing and sales improvement strategies for your business that don't cost you a fortune.

PART TWO:

Business Strategies To Generate More Sales and Increase Profits

CHAPTER 7

Capture Your Prospects Contact Info and Create a List Of Quality Leads

Capturing your leads and prospects contact information when they visit your business, website or call-in, must be the foundation of your business strategies. This simple concept is a powerful and effective strategy being used by many successful businesses all over the world, but for some reason, many Dental Practices allow prospects and leads to come in or call without even getting their name, email address or phone number.

Have you ever considered how powerful and profitable effective follow up campaigns can be to your business? Most good business owners know the truth of this strategy, but have never taken the time to implement it. Once you see how much money you are leaving on the table, you are going to kick yourself for not doing it sooner.

The other benefit of capturing your prospects contact information is you gain the peace of mind that comes with being able to generate sales at will. You no longer have to sit on the sidelines day after day while your business has little to no patients walking in the door.

However, just like many of the strategies revealed in this book, you must have proven and effective conversion scripts and systems in place to consistently and predictably get these patients back into your business to purchase from you.

Finally, you may be thinking that prospects are not willing to give you their contact information, but that is not true. The key to getting their contact information is to give them a special offer in exchange for them giving you their contact information. For example, you can offer to mail them out special promotions or offer to enter their name in a free prize giveaway. You can even offer to give them a free informative booklet in exchange for their contact information. Many of the biggest and most successful businesses in the world spend thousands of dollars building a list of prospects that may not be ready to buy from them today, because they know it means millions of dollars in profits in the future.

CHAPTER 8

How to Make Money With
Your Business Phone

Are you aware that you are probably losing a lot money every single day? How, you ask? By not having a proven and powerful phone answering script that's designed to capture your patients contact information or ask them to make a purchase over the phone, that's how.

Let me prove it to you. When someone calls your business asking for directions to your location, what do you give them? Directions, of course. Well, do you know if and when that person on the phone is planning on coming in? The answer is probably not.

However, what if you offered incoming phone call prospects the option to take advantage of the special sale you are having for today only for 5% - 10% off for first-time patients, if they come to your business today. Do you think that would give them an incentive to come into your business today? What about offering to put them on a mailing list for the next big promotions or sale that you are having? See, your priorities for every incoming phone call you receive from a prospect should be the following:

- Collect their name, phone and email address so you can add them to your follow-up campaign.
- Record the reason why they are calling as well as the products and services they are interested in, so you

33

know what your marketplace wants.

- If you have a product you can sell, offer them the option to purchase by phone, if they already know what they want.
- Get them to commit to coming into your business today by setting an appointment.

If you are truly seeking profitable success with your incoming phone calls, it is also important that you select and train the best staff person to answer your phone. I am fairly confident that you have someone on your staff that sounds nice, pleasant and professional on the phone and truly enjoys talking to patients. This is the type of person you want answering your phones on a daily basis. With a proven script, you will be surprised at how many prospects will give you a chance to earn their business simply because someone spoke nicely to them, captured their contact information and set an appointment.

You also will want to train this staff person to follow-up on outgoing calls to prospects and leads that are in your marketing funnel. Sometimes prospects just need to know that someone cares enough about their needs and wants, to make a little extra effort. This simple little strategy has paid huge rewards over the years for my clients, and it doesn't cost you one extra penny.

CHAPTER 9

Transform Your Patient Receipts into Marketing Ads & More Sales

When you go to the grocery business have you ever noticed that your receipts have coupons on them? Okay, the truth is that most men don't notice those types of things, but with women it is a different story. They collect the coupons so they can use them on their next purchase, but in reality those coupons are just receipts with an offer printed on them. Also, have you ever noticed when you go to a fast food restaurant that they offer to enter your name into a monthly drawing for a one thousand dollar prize if you call into a special number and leave your opinion and feedback?

Have you ever taken the time to think about these things from a business owner's point of view? The reason why these companies use these strategies is because these strategies generate more sales and profits. Grocery stores have been using this strategy for many years because their customers are accustomed to saving coupons and purchasing items which are on sale. The reason why businesses collect customer opinions and feedback is because it allows them to keep their pulse on the rapid changes in the marketplace, while also allowing them to see the areas of their business they need to improve or change.

However, most other businesses have yet to catch on to this profitable strategy. In fact, many business owners in other industries that hire me have never even considered the possibility of having a mini-ad, discount or coupon printed on their sales receipts. You can even have your refer-a-friend rewards program ad on the receipt. This transforms a useless piece of paper into a money-generating magnet, just by making a simple change.

You can also put an ad on your receipts highlighting your testimonial or customer feedback phone number. To do this just call your phone service provider and let them know that you want a voicemail only phone number. This extra voicemail phone number may only costs five or ten bucks a month, but the advantage is tremendous. By using this technique, you discover exactly what your patients want and their view of how their experience went. Once you get the testimonial, you can now use that in all your other advertising to prove to prospects that you are the best option in your market place which provides social proof that you are a leader in your industry.

CHAPTER 10

How to Make Money With Your Business Signs (Inside & Outside)

Some of the most valuable real estate in your Dental Practice is your business signage. If you have been in business any amount of time, then you already know that good business signage can be critical in helping patients find your business. However, have you ever thought about using business signage to actually attract prospects to your business?

When I talk about business signage, I am referring to signs on the outside of your business windows, as I assume your building signage is already completed and cannot be changed. Most of the window business signs owners' use usually says generic stuff like, "Sale," "Financing Terms Available," or "New Patients Welcome." In this day and time those types of signs are not worth the plastic they're printed on.

If you really want powerful and effective signs on the windows of your office, you must use signs that state your USP and draw patients in. For example: "FREE Report Reveals the Truth Concerning Common Misconceptions About Dental Care That Are Keeping You from a Healthy, Happy Smile You Can Be Proud Of". And then direct them to your website to download it!

The key to having business signage which attracts prospects and patients is to focus on the benefits that patients want. If you have no idea what the patients in your marketplace are looking for, then you need to ask every prospect that comes into your business and use that information to create a U.S.P. that attracts the right type of prospect.

37

Another place for you to focus on effective business signage that most businesses overlook is inside your business. Just because you got a prospect to walk into your business doesn't mean that your job is done. In your office, you must have signs that capture the prospects attention and compel them to ask you about it. Here's a quick test you can perform to see if you have good signage in your business: When is the last time a customer was in your business and pointed to a sign and asked you about that product/program/service/offer? If the answer is never or you cannot remember, then chances are that your in-business signage isn't working as effectively as it could be working.

Effective in- business signage can help your staff close a sale, remind patients of why they came into your business or keep a sale closed for you because patients are constantly reminded of your unique U.S.P.

Another concept here is to combine a unique new technology, QR code marketing (see image below). You will have one made that once scanned leads your prospect to the online location you set. This could be a special offer, text sign up or just your basic contact details like mine is below. I can help you with this if you get stuck.

CHAPTER 11

Mail Monthly Newsletters to Prospects and Mail Quarterly Newsletters to Past Patients

Most Dental Practices usually remember to run ads once in a while, but only a select few choose to mail out a quarterly or monthly newsletter to past patients and prospects. This simple little strategy has been responsible for billions of dollars in profits for small Dental Practices who choose to actually use this strategy in their business. Those who do not use this strategy, often wonder why their patients never come back to purchase from them after many hours of building rapport.

Using monthly or quarterly newsletters can literally mean the difference between struggling to pay your lease or mortgage each month and making a nice little profit on a slow month.

See, the truth is, no matter how much rapport you may have built with a prospect or patient at the time they were in your office or on the phone with you, the minute they walk out the door, anything and everything is fighting for their attention. They have spouses, children, jobs, relatives, vacations, shopping etc. They may have the best motives and intentions when you talk to them, but the longer you wait to follow up with them, the more they forget you.

Have you ever ran into a prospect or past customer at the grocery business or out in your local community who you felt should have really come back to buy from you, but when you ask them what ever happened, they tell you they went somewhere else? How did that make you feel? Well, why does that happen? Most of the time it happens because salespeople forget to follow up and you don't have a system in place to make sure that prospects never forget you.

You should be mailing out a promotional or educational/informative piece of literature to your prospects at least once a month or every two weeks. If you are not doing this, then you are losing money left and right to your competitors. However, your newsletter or promotional ad should be written to generate sales, not boring and stale. The only way to make sure that your newsletter or monthly marketing piece is good is by learning to be a good copywriter or using proven mail pieces and articles which are already proven to work or.

When it comes to sending your past patients your newsletter, you should quarterly and should focus on generating referrals and highlighting your loyalty rewards program. You should also put a promotion in your newsletter that rewards your past patients for coming in and purchasing additional products and services from you.

CHAPTER 12

Mail Monthly Offers to Your Past Prospects and Leads

Mailing monthly offers to your past prospects and leads must become as natural to you as breathing and eating. In an earlier chapter I presented the reasons why you should collect your prospects contact information, but collecting the contact information and getting sales from your list of prospects are two different things.

With this strategy, you can choose to include the offer in your newsletter like the previous chapter mentioned or you can send the offer separately. However, don't get stuck in procrastination mode debating what would work better, newsletter or separate offer. Just be sure to mail something every month.

Now, when you begin to consistently implement this strategy, you will begin to get a consistent and predictable flow of buying patients in your business. I'm always surprised at Dental Practices who think that they can make a reliable, consistent income based solely on referral business alone. Sure, getting referrals is great, but do you really control that process? No, of course not. However, when you mail your list, you can control the offer you are presenting to your list of prospects and past patients. You can even choose the day that you want your mail piece to go out to them, so in my experience it' is much better when a business owner controls your own success. So, to start you must hire a professional copywriter or personally create a series of sales, promotions and ads that you can use to automatically send out emails, postcards or letters to your prospects. You want them to think of your business when they are ready to make their purchase.

Your monthly mailers to your list of prospects and leads could be newsletters, coupons, informational booklets, emails and more. The only requirement you must meet with whatever you're mailing out is that it must be effective at generating sales and making you money. You are not trying to build a brand, because building a brand doesn't pay the mortgage. Only new patients and generating profits and depositing money in your bank account pays the mortgage.

CHAPTER 13

How to Host a Very Profitable Friends and Family Sale

The friends and family sale has long been used by the retail industry as a advertising tool to generate business. However, I have very rarely seen businesses outside of the retail industry use the strategy. Well, why not find a way to make this sale a part of your advertising strategies. After all, the chances are pretty good that your current patients know other people who are similar to them that could use your product or service.

However, before you run out and try this strategy I must give you a word of caution. See, over the years, I have noticed that if you run this sale the wrong way, then the friends and family sale will just be a huge flop. After much investigating and testing in my own business, I have come to the conclusion that the large majority of time when we promoted our friends and family sales, we mostly got prospects who would have bought days or weeks earlier if we would have just given them the discount earlier. This completely defeats the purpose of having the sale. In fact, we were only risking losing the customer and delaying our profits because we were discouraging the customer from buying today, so that they could get the better sale price later.

So, here's the solution. Create ads that clearly state that the prospect can only get the discount only if they bring friends and family (prospects) with them to the sale. You can even tier the discount to handsomely reward those prospects who bring more friends and family. For example, give a five percent discount if they bring one person, ten percent discount if they bring two, and a fifteen percent discount if they bring three and a whopping twenty percent discount if they bring four people.

However, the key to the entire sale is that the friends and family must fill out a simple little contact information form when they visit your office. You can even create a drawing that they are being entered into a contest to win prizes or cash. When you let them know why you're gathering the information, they will not feel as awkward giving you their information. At the very least, this allows you to build your marketing database, and you may even get a sale or two from the friends and families at the sale, but the benefit is that you get to grow your prospecting list.

Finally, make sure the terms of the friends and family sale are well laid out on your website or on the advertisement itself. This will allow your patients to really play the game to get a bargain for themselves, while bringing you plenty of potential prospects.

CHAPTER 14

Create a Series of Informative Workshops, Classes Or Events To Attract Prospects

One of the easiest ways to instantly generate profits and sales is to piggy-back off other successful ideas and strategies. When you ride the coat tails of other successful trends, you eliminate the learning curve and create instant success. Many financial advisors, money managers and even home supply stores like Home Depot and Lowes have been using the strategy of hosting workshops, classes and events for their prospects and patients for many years and it's a big lead generator for them. Many of their classes are booked to capacity and patients and prospects love it.

That's why I highly recommend creating your own type of lead generating and credibility-building workshops, classes or events. As long as you are creating relevant content that your prospects find valuable, easy to implement and entertaining, you will find this to be a successful strategy.

So, the first step is deciding how often you want to offer your workshops. My advice is to have a workshop at least once per quarter. This allows your prospects to develop a relationship with you while also building your credibility in the eyes of your marketplace. Secondly, decide how long you want your workshops to last. The best length for most businesses would range from sixty to ninety minutes. Once you decide that, then you can begin putting together an outline of the type of information that you would want to give away to your prospects in your workshops. You can choose from several various formats for your workshop. Here are some examples:

- Question & Answer
- Interview The Expert
- Do-It-Yourself Teeth Whitening
- Product Demonstration

Regardless of the format that you choose, just be sure that the content is relevant, useful and fairly fresh to your marketplace.

After you decide the frequency, length and format of your workshops, the next step is deciding the location and delivery method. There are several different formats you can use to do this depending on your business model. Here are some examples:

- Video – Buy an inexpensive video recorder and film yourself doing your workshop. Then, use a service like Youtube.com to post your video to a special page on your website. Remember to advertise your online video workshop in your regular marketing efforts.

- In-office Presentations – This is when you have the prospects come to your business location to listen and watch your informative presentation.

- Teleseminars – With this strategy you get a teleconference phone number and have prospects call in on a certain day and time.

- Audio CD – You can record your workshop using software on your computer and then burn copies to a disc. Then, mail them out to your list of prospects.

- Webinars – You can use a service that records your computer screen while you are providing information using a PowerPoint slide presentation. Let me know if you need a recommendation to an all-in-one technology I use that is extremely affordable.

It's important to remember that this strategy can only be effective if you advertise them aggressively and if your content is relevant to your marketplace. The other good thing about this strategy is that you can really attract the attention of the local media by submitting regularly scheduled press releases and doing email campaigns and feature spots in your monthly and quarterly newsletters for your workshop, class or event. All in all, you can really generate some massive publicity and quality leads by implementing this strategy.

CHAPTER 15

How to Transform Your Patients into Walking Billboards For Your Business

Whenever someone makes a new purchase, one of the first things they do is brag to their family, friends and neighbors. Your goal in using this strategy is to tap into that excitement and leverage it to create new patients. I like to call this strategy the radius marketing strategy. By using the radius marketing strategy, you can capture that excitement and gain access to new patients. Secondly, most people tend to have friends with similar interests who live in the same neighborhoods. So, when you have a customer who comes into your business and makes a purchase, chances are that their neighborhood is filled with other prospects that would also be able to afford and appreciate your products or services.

In order to use this strategy, you simply take the address of a recent customer and draw an imaginary circle around their house which represents an actual distance of five blocks to ten blocks. Once you have your circle drawn, then you mail out a campaign to those prospects inside of your circle, because those are the neighbors of your current customer. The theme of the campaign is focused around teasing your prospects by revealing that someone in their neighborhood bought from you, so they should as well. You will also offer them a special neighborhood discount because they live in the same area as a current customer. You can map out the addresses close to your current customer and mail them automatically online at the website of the United States Parcel Service.

Let's examine a campaign:

- Patient purchases from you, so you go online and purchase a list of addresses of their neighbors.

- Write, create or purchase a series of three to seven mailers consisting of postcards, letters and discount coupons. (You can even set up an automated postcard or greeting card campaign that with a few mouse clicks a sequence of cards are automatically sent out to the list! Visit www.MarketingHuddleCards.com to find out more details.)

- Provide information on your mailers that direct the prospects to a special website specifically designed for neighbors of current patients to capture their email address and offer an incentive to get prospects to set an appointment to visit your business.

CHAPTER 16

Dialing For Dollars:
Using Telemarketing To
Grow Your Business

I n a previous chapter I revealed several ways that you or your staff can increase your sales, appointments and overall sale opportunities by changing the way you answer your business phone. In this chapter, I will discuss the tried and true method of generating prospects and patients using telemarketing. In recent years, telemarketing has gotten a bad reputation because of a few bad companies misusing the technique; however, it is still a very effective marketing strategy when used properly.

There are three important parts to effectively using telemarketing to generate business. The first important key to your success with telemarketing is your list of prospects that you are calling. Your success using this strategy is directly determined by your ability to contact the right type of prospect in the first place. The easiest way to do this is to use your current customer receipts and surveys to discover all of the information about your best patients. Then you can use that information to compile a customer profile. After you have created a customer profile, then it is time to create your list. This can be done by calling a company like Infousa.com or Usadata.com and asking them to compile a list of prospects who match the same criteria as your ideal customer profile.

Once you have a list of prospects to call, then your next step is to create an effective phone script. However, in order to create an effective phone script, you have to determine what the goal of your sales call will be. You can choose to write a phone script that sells your product over the phone or you can use the phone script to set appointments for prospect's to come into your business...or just to send them your free report on a specific dental topic. After you determine the goal of your phone call, then you need to record or write down the transcript of a face-to-face presentation that you or your sales staff has recently conducted. This will allow you to use a proven sales script when you are on the phone with prospects.

The last step in an effective telemarketing campaign is your ability and willingness to follow up with your prospects on a regular basis. When it comes to telemarketing, you must be willing to call weekly, monthly or even daily in some cases in order to have a chance to earn their business.

Following these three key ingredients will give your telemarketing campaign a great chance for success. Without using the key ingredients I listed for you, your telemarketing campaign will most likely be doomed to fail before you even begin. If done properly, telemarketing could be another tool that you have in your arsenal that can help drive prospects into your business.

CHAPTER 17

Follow The Yellow Brick Road: Yellow Page Advertising

In this age of domination by companies that use online marketing, it's hard to imagine that advertising in the yellow pages is still effective, but it is. It seems that everyone is singing the praises of the tremendous impact that marketing on the internet has, but there are still many prospects that prefer to use the yellow pages. These are the people who have spent twenty, thirty or forty years using the Yellow Pages phonebook to look up a product or service, so the habit is hard to change.

The yellow pages are especially important when it comes to finding a local service business. See, the down side of the Internet is that it is sometimes difficult to find a local company because the local company is competing with millions of other company websites. In those cases, a prospect may start by searching online, but then quickly decides to use the yellow pages because they are practically guaranteed to find a local service provider. This means that you MAY also continue to use the yellow pages as a place to advertiser your business. However, you must create an ad that makes your ad stick out and compels the prospect to call or visit your business. The keys to creating an ad that generates leads and prospects are pretty much the same as I listed in previous chapters:

1. Use headlines that attract patients.
2. Always have a compelling offer.

3. Insert testimonials from past patients.
4. Include a guarantee on your products and services.
5. Your ad must look unique and stand out from your competitors.
6. Your ad must ONLY focus on what your customer wants.
7. Have only one goal for each ad, which is to get patients to visit your business...or download your FREE REPORT from your website.
8. Tell the reason why you're offering the sale.
9. Write ads that are straight to the point and easy to understand.
10. Include QR codes to capture attention!

CHAPTER 18

The Holy Grail of Marketing: Generating Referrals

While every Dental Practice loves to get referrals, very few have a system in place to consistently generate those referrals. As you probably already know, referrals close at higher rate than most other types of leads, so if you want to take your business to the next level, you should definitely create a system that generates referrals.

In this chapter, I will give you a referral generation plan that will be easy, simple and powerful. However, you should know that there are several key components to creating an effective referral campaign. The first step in creating a powerful referral campaign is to have a product or service that is worth referring. Your product and service must be memorable and perform exactly as it is supposed to, in order for your patients to refer their friends and family to your business. If you have a crappy product that doesn't hold up over time or if you have a service that causes more problems that it solves, then it will be very difficult for the few patients you get to refer others to you.

The second step in creating a referral system is to build your request for referrals into your closing process. However, I am not saying that you should ask for referrals before you close the sale. You should ask for referrals after a customer had decided to buy, but before they leave your business. So, for example, when you have a patient in front of you then that moment is the perfect time to ask them if they know of anyone who also needs a new dentist. If they say yes, you then ask for permission to contact that referral and use the referring person's name.

TIP:
Think of some easy and affordable prizes to give away each month for the person who sends in the most referrals, or a smaller gift for EACH referral sent!

The last and final component to a successful referral campaign is to find a way to easily and automatically contact your patients and remind them to send you referrals. The best way that I've discovered to accomplish this is by inserting your patients into a monthly or quarterly mailing campaign that is designed to generate referrals. This can be a series of postcards, letters or phone calls that reminds them that you build your business by getting referrals from past patients. Just make sure that whatever method you choose, be sure to do it consistently with all your patients....and reward the patients who do refer, even if the referral does NOT lead to a sale!

CHAPTER 19

The Powerful Profit Potential
Of Packaging Your Products
And Services

Most businesses in the retail industry have long profited from this strategy, but most service providers neglect to use this strategy to its fullest potential. Packaging your products and services into bundles allows you to charge higher prices and creating the perception in the market place that you are a premium product or service provider. The packaging strategy allows you to promote and advertise several other products while initially getting patients to come into your business to purchase other products or services. This dramatically reduces your marketing costs because you are essentially piggy-backing on your current advertising efforts.

For example, could you offer a 3-pack tooth cleaning or whitening package? You could even have a premium package that includes extra features or tooth-care products you sell. See, in this case, you are already in front of the customer for one service, so why not offer them a valuable package that would entice them to purchase more from you.

The one thing that I would caution you to watch out for with this strategy, is the temptation to lower your prices to the point where you are making peanuts for profits and developing a reputation for being the cheapest dentist in your area. Even in the most competitive marketplaces you can package your products and services in a way that will allow you to charge a premium price.

CHAPTER 20

How Many Ways Can You Sell?
The Upsell, Cross Sell
and Downsell

When you get a prospect who says they are ready to purchase do you or your staff hurriedly write up the order and process the payment because you are afraid they will change their mind? How many times have you had someone take the time to visit your business, sit through a sales presentation, only to say they want to go and think about it. Well, these are two cases in which you have an alternative option that could result in bigger profits.

If you are like most businesses I consult with, then you probably just process the payment when a customer says they want to buy and let a customer walk when they say they want to go home and think about it. However, I guarantee you that if you are doing those two things, then you are missing out on a ton of cash.

The key to turning the regular sale into a spectacular sale is to have an option for the customer to instantly get more/bigger/better at a great value because they are buying right now. There have been companies who have increased the average amount of the order by 50% or more, just by having an upsell and a cross-sell. What add-on service can you have your staff ALWAYS recommend to every patient? Just like McDonalds who asks: "Would you like fries with that?"

Now, the downsell is when you have met with a patient and they chose not to buy a specific product or service. In this case, you can offer a scaled down version of the product or service for a cheaper price. This works really well when you attract patients to your business based on a package of products or services and as they raise objections, you can begin to strip the package apart and offer single items or services for a reduced price.

These strategies have been proven to work for thousands of companies who have chose to implement these profit building systems. Now, it's time for you to harness the power of these strategies too.

Can you take a look at you additional services that you offer and put them into packages to offer as a bundle as we discussed in the previous chapter, and then have a simple strategy to up-sell or down-sell a patient you are working with? It will only take a few minutes to put this together but it will be a great profit increase to your practice!

CHAPTER 21

Partnering With Other Businesses That Sell Complimentary Products and Services

Partnering with other businesses to promote your business is a joint venture strategy that few Dental Practices ever consider. It's probably because this joint venture strategy will require you to be really confident and comfortable in your own business. Otherwise, it would seem like you are risking losing your patients to another business, but that is not true. The key to this strategy is partnering with companies that don't sell the same types of products or services that you sell. Now, just to be clear about this strategy; you will not be exchanging the addresses of your patients with other businesses, you will be creating a in-business coupon or referral program that other businesses will give out to their patients or prospects.

When you partner with other businesses who sell complementary products and services to the same target market that you do, it allows you to gain access to your joint venture partner's patients who may be in the market for products or services you sell. Now, when I say partner with these other businesses, what I mean is to work out a mutually beneficial relationship with them. For example, you could host an informative workshop together and both of you send out a mailer to your list of past patients and both of you share the costs of the mailer and event location.

If you are having a problem coming up with some potential joint venture partners, here are a few questions to get the ball rolling:

- What other business or services sell related services to your patients?
- What other related products or services do your patients need that you don't have the ability to sell them?

This strategy can be really profitable, but also fun as well because you are teaming up with another business. It also creates accountability so that it actually gets done!

CHAPTER 22

Profitable Partnerships:
Partner With Your Patients

Out of all the joint venture strategies I know, the most important joint venture strategy is the one that includes your patients. Many companies call this a referral strategy, but I think of it as a referral strategy and a joint venture strategy. See, if you are rewarding your customer with the right incentives, they will work their butts off for your success.

The best joint venture strategy I've seen with patients involved is the referral bucks program. With this program you reward your past patients with business bucks for referring someone who purchases over a certain amount in your business and mentions your customer's name as the referring party. If you structure your program this way, then your patients will begin to pre-qualify the friends and people that they refer to you.

This is a powerful strategy, but only if you are providing a quality product and good service. It's also powerful because you can train your patients to buy from you in certain dollar amounts to qualify for certain rewards. This allows you to influence your average purchase amount, which then allows you to increase your profit margins.

It always amazes me that more businesses don't use this strategy. It really is a great program when applied correctly. If you want to take it up a notch then send each one of your patients ten or twenty referral cards which look like business cards, but it has a blank spot for them to write their name and phone number on it. You may also want to include a special discount coupon on the card, so that their referral would be sure to give the referring patients' name when visiting your business. This way you train your patients to always be on the lookout for referrals, because it actually pays for them to refer people to you. You may also want to max your referral bucks at a specific amount that can be redeemed for each purchase once your program gets rolling along.

You can even partner with another local business to have them provide the patients of your Dental Practice with a special discount or offer. This way you create a way to give something that doesn't cost you anything…and you can offer the same to THEIR customers as well!

PART THREE:

Online & Internet Strategies That Generate Tons of Prospects and Patients

CHAPTER 23

Build a Website That Actually Generates Sale

Imagine waking up at 7 am in the morning and already having had three appointments that were booked during the night and a couple of your dental products sold! That's the feeling you can experience on a daily basis once you create an effective website for your business. Now, when I say effective website, I am NOT talking about just having a "pretty brochure" website for your friends and family members to compliment you on. I'm talking about a website that generates leads and automatically transforms visitors into buying patients.

In this chapter I will give you some direction on the steps you must take in order to transform your website expense into a stream of revenue.

The first component of a successful website is making sure that your website looks professional and clearly shows your products, services, prices, specs and contact phone number and directions to your business. There is nothing more frustrating than having to search all over a website to find a phone number or office address. If you have a reputable business, then you should post as much information on your website about your products and services as possible.

Secondly, your website must have an opt-in form to capture your prospects email address. You have probably seen this email opt-in form on other websites that you frequent. An opt-in form is a place on your website that asks a website visitor for their email address in exchange for something like a free report, discount coupon or newsletter subscription. However, you must offer highly desirable "lead bait" in exchange for a prospect's email address. When it comes to lead bait, it's important that your prospects view your offer as valuable and are willing to give you their email address, your lead bait can be just about anything.

Third, your website must have a method to connect with website visitors in a personal way. You can use video, audio or a simple head shot photo on the home page which gives the website visitor a personalized greeting from you. The video can be recorded with a simple digital camera and then uploaded to YouTube.com. Once it's on YouTube, you can then put the video on your website. If you already have a website, then you can get your web designer and tech guy to make all of these specific changes.

The fourth change should be making sure you have emails pre-programmed into your website, which are automatically sent out to prospects who signed up to receive your bait. By pre-programming your emails, it appears as if you are following up with every prospect personally. This will give you the ability to follow up with your leads automatically for as long as you want. One of the largest and most affordable services that provide this service can be found at www.MarketingHuddle.Aweber.com

These are just a few of the major changes which should be made to your website in order to convert prospects into patients. There are many more changes, but the one principle you need to remember is this: Hire an experienced marketer to design your website to sell. Don't make the mistake of allowing a graphic designer or tech guy design your website without the input and guidance of an experienced marketer. Otherwise, you will have a beautiful website that never makes you a dime.

CHAPTER 24

Increasing Patients
with
Pay Per Click

Most Dental Practices realize the benefits of website marketing, but many owners do little to nothing to get their website in front of prospective patients on a consistent basis. See, having a website built for your business and getting your website up and running online is only the first step. However, your website won't make you one measly sale, if you are not able to get it in front of prospective patients who are willing, ready and able to spend money to purchase your products or services.

There are dozens of strategies to generate leads and prospects online, but in the next several chapters, I will cover the most profitable and easy to set up strategies that I have come across in my years of internet marketing.

One of the cheapest and quickest strategies to get up and running is the pay per click strategy. If you haven't heard of pay per click before, then let me give you a brief overview.

When you visit a search engine website like Google.com and type in a word or phrase and click enter, you will see a webpage which shows the results of the search you entered. On the very top of the page you will see two or three search results that will be highlighted in a shaded box that has a different color than the rest of the page. On the far right of the webpage you will also notice a row of eight to ten ads. The ads at the top and right of the search results page are ads placed there by companies who pay anywhere from five cents to five dollars to show up as an advertiser for a specific word. However, they only pay the fee if a potential customer clicks on the ad. There is also a bidding component to pay per click, which means that many advertisers are bidding a certain amount to be near the top of the list of advertisers on the search results webpage.

Using pay per click is such a powerful strategy that many million dollar companies have been built on the back of this one strategy. However, there are several key components to this strategy which must be in place to turn it into a money maker for your business.

The keys to success when using pay per click are:

- Bid in amounts until you get really good at it.

- Write a compelling ad which attracts the right type of prospective customer.

- Have a special website designed specifically for your pay per click campaign. Your normal website will not make you one penny in most cases if you just plug it into your pay per click campaign.

- Hire an expert pay per click manager if you can't get the hang of it.

CHAPTER 25

Writing and Submitting Informative & Educational Articles Online

When patients begin shopping for a dentist, they often start by finding as much information as possible online.

In order to make a good impression on the prospect that is doing their research and homework, you have to make sure that you are putting your business information in a place where consumers will easily find it. There is no better way to do this than by writing informative and educational articles and having them posted on websites where your target prospects are likely to be searching.

Writing and submitting articles to online directories allows you to really control the flow of information about your products and services in your local market. I have had tremendous success using short articles containing about four to five hundred words to generate leads and prospects. You don't have to be the next Tom Clancy or Stephen King in order to get prospects to read your articles. All you have to do is write a short couple of paragraphs about a particular promotion that you currently are advertising.

The subject of the articles should be educational but also slightly entertaining. The last thing you want to be is boring and sounding like you are writing a users manual. Consumers want to know that your products, services and business will provide a good quality product, but consumers also like to work with businesses that are fun, exciting and helpful.

If you are a pretty good writer, you can write your own articles to promote your business, however, I strongly suggest hiring a freelance writer to submit one or two articles per month on your behalf to the top ten or twenty online directories.

Writing and submitting articles to online directories will help to boost your rankings in popular search engines like Google.com and Yahoo.com. These search engines will give your website higher priority when a prospect types in a keyword and will give you a better chance to you to show up as one of the first ten choices in your target market. This is because each article on a directory with properly formatted keywords linked to your website will provide you a strong backlink. Google ranks the websites with the most authority and content and this is a great way to accomplish this.

CHAPTER 26

Partnering Online with Other Websites

If having a website that actually generates leads is a rare thing for a Dental Practice, then partnering with other websites to swap or purchase advertising space must seem next to impossible. However, once you have a website that attracts your target customer, then partnering with other websites to help each other generate patients is not that far of a reach. This is another strategy which seems intimidating on the surface level, but once you get started, it's actually pretty simple.

Obviously this strategy requires that you have a website; however, there is another step you must complete before implementing this strategy. The first step is having a graphic designer create several various size web banners for you to market your business on other websites. The next step is making sure that you can actually post ads on your website. Or have your webmaster or tech guy post them online. Once this step is done, you can them move on to implementing the strategy.

The easiest way to implement this strategy is to start by researching the local businesses that you currently use on an ongoing basis. The first step you should do is visit online search engine Google.com and enter their business name and find out if they even have a website. If they have a website that looks decent then visit their business just like normal and speak to the owner or the person in charge of marketing and introduce yourself. If you are not recognized by anyone, then let them know that you are a regular customer.

Once you have introduced yourself, let them know that you have a website and you would like to do an ad swap with them. Let them know that you will promote their business for free on your website, but you would like free advertising on their website as well. This should be enough of a hook for a semi-intelligent business owner to move forward with the partnership. However, if they don't bite on this, then just move on to the next local business that you frequent and make the same offer.

There are two key notes to mention when using this strategy. The first key is make sure you have tracking software installed on your website, so you will know exactly which advertising partner each prospect is coming from. Secondly, make sure the prospect is redirected to a specific webpage that is optimized to sell these types of patients. Your website manager should know how to do both of these fairly easily.

CHAPTER 27

Guarantee That Prospects Find You Online and Not Your Competitors

Most of the time, having a beautiful website that highlights your products, services, office and staff is a wonderful and necessary marketing tool. However, you will never make a single penny from your website if prospective patients cannot find your website online.

Every Dental Practice I consult with knows that they need a website, but virtually none know how to guarantee that their prospective patients find their website before finding their competitors website. So in this chapter I will reveal how you can practically guarantee that your prospects find your website before your competitors.

Having a general idea about how search engines work is the first step in making sure prospects can find your website online. Search engines are websites like Google.com, Yahoo.com and Bing.com. These websites compile tons of data and information and make sifting through it manageable by organizing it by order of importance to the "keyword" you typed into your browser. For example, if you type in "pizza restaurants in Milford, CT" into your search engine browser, then you will get the most relevant pizza restaurants in Milford, CT that your search engine feels ranks most closely to the phrase or keyword term you typed in. That's why you want your website and the pages on your website to match as closely to the relevant terms for your target market as possible.

Understanding how prospects search online is the second thing you must understand in order to ensure that prospects find your website. For example, if a customer is looking for a dentist in Chicago, then you need to have a webpage on your website that is especially designed for those types of patients. The simplest way to think of this concept is by focusing on "buyer keywords."

Buyer keywords are words that prospects type into their search engine browser to find places to buy the product or service they are looking for. For example, if you were a furniture store owner, who do you think is a more serious prospect: the customer who types in "sofa bed sales for memorial weekend," or the customer who types in "sofa bed"? So, if you had to choose between designing a webpage on your website for generic sofabeds or designing a specific webpage for sofa bed sales for memorial weekend, which one should you choose? Apply this same logic for your Dental Practice, what would your prospective patients be searching for when they are really looking to change dentists?

CHAPTER 28

Advertise Your Website URL on Everything in Your Business

Promoting the heck out of your website is one very effective but underrated online strategy that can have a dramatic impact on your bottom line. As I already established in early chapters, just having a website and putting it online is not enough to get money in your bank account. Many Dental Practices I consult with are under the false impression that having a website is the savior of their business and business. This couldn't be further from the truth.

In today's technologically advanced culture, having a website is simply mandatory. In fact, you are viewed as a dinosaur if you do not have website. From a customer's perspective, having a website is not seen as a huge advantage. From a customer's perspective every business should have a website.

It's best to view your website as a separate tool that you could use to generate sales, instead of viewing it as the answer to all your sales woes. After all, it's not the website that sets you apart; it is about your USP and your ability to consistently attract patients to your website. Once you get prospects to your website, your next job is to actually write words and use images on your website that compel your customer to open their wallet, take out their credit card and purchase from you.

Your website address should be advertised on your business cards, sales receipts, business windows, business signage and anywhere else you can think of. This strategy works even better if you have a memorable website address. The important key is to remember that your website does nothing for you unless you get visitors to your website and then are able to convert them into patients.

CHAPTER 29

Harnessing the Power of Craigslist.com to Boost Your Dental Practice.

In the last decade, patients purchasing products online have accounted for tens of billions of dollars in sales. However, millions of those dollars have changed hands as a direct result of having been seen on a popular website Craigslist.com. In fact, every month millions of Americans shop online at the popular free website called Craigslist.com. One of my most popular strategies for a business that sells a product consists of advertising your entry level, slightly damaged or discontinued products online for reduced prices on Craigslist. This would allow you generate profits from products that traditionally just sits in your warehouse for months or years and collects dust.

The best part about Craigslist.com is the fact that it's free to advertise unlimited products on the website. The biggest obstacle you will face when advertising on Craigslist.com is the uploading of images and writing descriptions about the products you are selling. However, you can have one of your staff members specialize in posting your listings on the website on a daily basis, so you don't personally have to do the work.

You may think this is a strange strategy, but think about it…how many other dentists advertise on Craigslist? See what I mean? You will spend a little time, no money…but have little competition!

CHAPTER 30

Listing Your Dental Practice In
Highly Visible Online Directories

Have you ever been searching for a product and service online that you felt should have been easy to find, but were unable to find it? How did that make you feel? You probably felt frustrated and maybe even gave up and changed your mind on using the product or service. Well, that's exactly the feeling that you want your prospects to avoid. One of the ways to make sure that this doesn't happen is to make sure your business is listed on every possible online directory.

In order for you to understand the importance of listing your business in all relevant online business directories, you first need to understand how patients may find your business online. See, over the last couple of years, small Dental Practices has been told that prospects no longer use the physical phone book or yellow pages to locate businesses. However, there are some prospects that still check the phone book when looking for certain types of businesses.

The same rule applies when prospects are searching online. While Google, Yahoo and Bing control over 75% of the search engine market, millions of prospect still use online business directories like Yelp, Super Yellow Pages and various other online directories to find consumer friendly business with a track record of quality and high levels of customer service. In order to find a comprehensive list of online business directories, visit your preferred search engine and type in the keyword "online business directories."

77

CHAPTER 31

The Proven Power Of
Email Marketing

Over the past several years, having a website has become the standard expectation of successful s business. Most Dental Practices have either purchased a website or have a simple webpage that directs visitors to their business. However, less than one percent of small to medium businesses utilize effective email marketing campaigns to give patients incentives to purchase from their businesses after their initial visit to the website or office. Neglecting to implement an effective email marketing campaign is the same as leaving thousands of dollars lying around on the ground each month.

Since I've began helping Dental Practices increase their sales and profits, I have discovered the reason why so many Dental Practices miss out on the easy profits from their website. The number one reason for missing out on the easy profits is because they do not actually get their prospects or patients email address. If you never have the email address then you cannot possibly use it to market to your prospects and past patients.

When I say email marketing, I'm not just talking about collecting email addresses of patients who have emailed you with questions, because most times that doesn't really happen. In order to have an effective email marketing campaign, you must have enticing bait that patients will get in exchange for giving you their email address. For example, your "email bait" could be a coupon, rewards program or a simple informative report titled, "7 Insider Strategies to Choosing a New Dentist" or a similar title. In order to capture the email address you can use a service that I recommend by visiting www.marketinghuddle.aweber.com

Once you have the email address you can then send out emails about sales, promotions or informative and educational tips. However, you cannot just send out emails begging prospects or patients to buy. Your emails must be fun, educational and timely. Therefore, unless you are a professional writer and marketer, you will want to hire a professional marketer to write your emails and suggest the best frequency to send them out.

TIP:
Consider increasing the effectiveness of your emails by sending video emails. I use a simple service that not only does this but also lets you send video auto-responders to automatically follow up. You can learn more here: www.TotalVideoEmail.com

CHAPTER 32

Creating a Weekly or Monthly
Online Newsletter

I f you truly want to explode your profits and sales in your business, then get out of the salesman mentality and get into the relationship building mentality.

When you began to see your prospects and patients as people who can become your friends and extended family, you will treat them differently. Many times a patient becomes irate and cancels an appointment simply because the receptionist treated them with a cold detached manner, instead of talking to them as a friend. Building relationships with your patients has to be your number one priority if you want to create patients for life.

One of the ways in which you can build a relationship with your prospects and patients is by sending out fun, education and entertaining newsletters once per month/quarter. At a minimum you should send out the newsletters once a quarter to your past patients and once a month to your prospects that you've collected email addresses from.

It is very important that the content of your newsletter be natural and not too well polished. The reality is, the more down to earth and simple your newsletter is, the more patients will be able to relate to you through your newsletter. In fact, the last thing you want to do is create a slick looking newsletter that uses words, phrases and pictures that are nothing like what you would actually say or do. Remember, this is about building a relationship with you and your business. It's not about putting out the most professional newsletter on the planet.

The content of your newsletter should include pictures of you and your staff. You should also include pictures of your patients having fun or purchasing in your business. It is also a good idea to include a contest or sweepstakes which rewards patients for reading the newsletter and answering hidden questions in the newsletter. You also want the newsletter to be laid back and not just industry jargon and talk. Most of your patients don't know industry jargon and don't care about it, but they do care about their pets, gardening and recipes. As silly as it sounds, you want your newsletter to be written for the normal guy and gal. Of course, you want to put a section promoting your products and services too, but that should be a small percentage of your newsletter.

PART FOUR:

Publicity Strategies That Generate Huge Profits at Little to No Cost

CHAPTER 33

Writing Articles for Magazines and Newspapers

The perfect marketing plan should include both paid advertising strategies and free publicity strategies. In fact, free publicity marketing strategies are much more effective in promoting your business than 99% of paid marketing strategies. However, you need both strategies in order to provide a constant stream of growth and profits.

One of the best methods you can use to generate tons of free publicity for your business without coming across as a pushy salesperson, is writing articles for newspapers or magazines. This strategy can pay huge dividends especially when you become as the "go-to" expert for a publication that your target market reads on a regular basis.

Writing articles for magazines and newspapers not only gets you recognition from your target market, but this strategy also helps you become a magnet for other free publicity opportunities. It is a great feeling to have prospects visit your business and buy from you because you are the expert in your niche. That feeling is a lot different than having people shop your prices all over town, visit your business and receive excellent service from you, but then go and buy from somewhere else because the other business was ten cents cheaper. The best way to avoid being shopped to death is to become the obvious go-to expert for your niche.

The reason why writing articles for magazines and newspapers works so well is because we are all taught from a young age to believe what the newspapers tell us. The majority of people in our culture believe news stories as if they are the gospel. When you become part of the experts that the newspapers and magazines rely on for their information, then you become known as the expert. Your patients will begin to believe everything you tell them as factual and truthful instead of questioning your every little move and decision.

The best way to get your articles included in a newspaper or magazine is to write three to twelve articles and have them professionally edited. You can then contact your local newspaper or target magazines and offer to be a guest writer or offer your articles for inclusion in their publication.

CHAPTER 34

Using Press Releases to Generate Sales

Writing press releases is the quickest and easiest way to get local and national media outlets to notice and promote your business. Unfortunately, most Dental Practices only think about using a press release with a grand opening. However, you should be sending out a press release at least once a month, but only if you have a marketing plan that includes professionally prepared press releases which are informative, educational and entertaining.

By this point, you may be asking yourself why local and nation media would be interested in your business. Well, the truth of the matter is that radio, newspaper and television stations all need news stories on a regular basis. Media outlets must have enough news to fill their air time and pages of their newspapers. Without stories to talk about newspapers, magazines and news reports become very boring and mundane.

If you implement a regular press release campaign in your business, you will begin to get offers to be in your local media. Over time you will become a local celebrity in your target market, and that will allow you to attract prospects to your business because they want to be associated with a celebrity who is successful.

Just like with many of the other strategies, your press release strategy can only work effectively if hire a marketing-minded writer or become a good marketing-minded writer who knows how to write in a way that compels prospects to actually take the necessary action and visit your business. Do not make the mistake of thinking that any press release will be good enough. You must either learn the skill of copywriting or hire a professional copywriter to create your compelling press releases. Also, don't forget to distribute them online for more reach and backlinks to your website! When your press release is published in an online newspaper, even if it's in an area you do not practice in, the readers may just know a family member in your area or be relocating there soon themselves.

At the time of this writing, I just watched a news story on the history of Home Depot and in their early years they had people driving 2 hours to come to their store! This was because a family member read a news story and called them up on the phone to tell them about the Home Depot sale. That is the power of media, and these days it is as easy as a mouse-click!

CHAPTER 35

Sponsor Local Charity Events

Sponsoring local charity events is another great strategy to build up goodwill towards your business while getting your message across to your target market. Sponsoring local charity events is not a new strategy, but it hasn't really been embraced on a larger scale by many small to medium businesses. However, now that you know about this highly effective strategy, you can reap the rewards of implementing it into your business.

The key to profiting from sponsorship of local charity events is to hone in on your target market and discover what charity events they will be most interested in attending. This requires you to gather information from your target market, which you cannot do unless you ask your patients for their input on your website or in your business.

Once you gather information from your past and current patients, then you can begin to look for sponsorship opportunities that match your target market. There are thousands of sponsorship opportunities in your local area. The fastest way to find a sponsorship opportunity is to contact non-profit organizations which match your target markets interests.

It is important for you to know that sponsorship opportunities will require an investment from your business ranging from a few hundred dollars to several thousand dollars. Most sponsorship opportunities will have various levels, so don't worry about being locked into a huge expensive contract.

When deciding on a specific non-profit organization or cause to champion, make sure that your business and businesses receive maximum coverage on the specific organizations website and marketing material. Remember that the goal of your sponsorship opportunities is to bring exposure to your businesses.

However, you can choose a charity event that has significance to you, but just make sure that it serves dual purposes, otherwise it will make you feel really good, but won't generate the desired amount of free publicity for your business.

You don't have to make it overtly a sales mission either. Just getting out in the local community will work wonders to bring exposure to your Dental Practice. And don't forget to announce each event on your website and social media sites like Facebook and Twitter. (you ARE on Facebook and Twitter, right?!).

When you do this, send the links over to the charity or event so they know you are helping them out, who knows, you may get a link back from their website to yours!

CHAPTER 36

Run Your Sales &
Promotions Around Holiday's

One of the oldest marketing tricks in the book is to design your marketing campaigns around holiday promotions. Yet, most Dental Practices do very few strategic marketing campaigns to make the most of the holiday sale tradition in the marketplace and this means they leave thousands of dollars in profit on the table each and every year.

The first step you must do before you even consider maximizing this strategy is create a marketing calendar. Once you have created a marketing calendar you will have a blueprint to follow each month. Each and every month you should have sale or promotion which is fueled by free publicity strategies and paid advertising strategies. Remember to focus on the "off-holidays" such as "groundhog day" or "friend day" etc. These will set you apart from everyone else running a 4th of July special!

After you have completed your first step of establishing a twelve month marketing calendar, your next step is to plan out exactly what the sale offer will be. Some sales should be percentage discounts, but some sales should be packages with something given for free in exchange for making a purchase.

The last and final step is to remember to set up a marketing campaign consisting of several methods of communicating with your prospects. For example, you can send out postcards, letters, emails and pre-recorded phone messages. Most times it takes contacting a customer several times before they can actually make a buying decision.

CHAPTER 37

Create A Television Show on the Internet!

While marketing to your past patients is the easiest way to find easy-to-close prospects, being on television is a great way to reach many more new prospects. Just imagine the audience you could reach if you could be on television. Well, in this current economic market, advertising your business on television could definitely be expensive! But it doesn't have to cost you a penny.

One of the best kept secrets in advertising is the power of using online live broadcasting in your target market to reach prospects at little to no money out of pocket. The reason for the secrecy is mostly because big ad agencies can't charge you exorbitant fees to recommend this resource to you. You should look into ustream.tv to see if this is an option to explore for you.

While there is typically no monetary cost to being online, there are some requirements that you must meet in order to take advantage of these incredible resource. The first major requirement is that you must create a twenty five to thirty minute program which can be aired several times a week, or at least a series of topics that you could cover in a show live. The program you create must be educational and informative to the audience.

My suggestion would be to partner with other local business to create a local expert panel show. The products on the show could come from your business, but the advice would come from the expert panel you would bring together. You

90

could even shoot in your own business using simple camera equipment you can find on Amazon for under $200.

The second requirement is you should not blatantly advertise your business or product when you are on-air. This may seem like a huge problem, but it's really not that big of a deal. All you have to do is create a program which educates people and mention where people can reach you for more information. You can probably even create a special website just for your program that isn't a hard selling website, but will give information about where you operate your business from.

CHAPTER 38

Write a Book That Positions You as The Go-To Expert In Your Niche

One of the little known hidden secrets of building a business that is recession proof, is establishing yourself as the go-to expert for your niche. One of the best ways I know to accomplish this is by writing a book especially for your target market.

Every dentist would love to find the easy patient who is ready to buy the instant they walk through the door. However, the large majority of patients need days and weeks of gathering information before they make a decision. If you can find a way to become a part of your prospects decision making process when they are searching for information, you will become the expert they learn to rely on. Once you become their familiar expert, the price haggling stops and prospects call or come into your business ready to purchase.

One of the fastest ways to build instant credibility with your target market is to write a book. Writing a book to educate and help your target market, automatically gives you a huge advantage over your competitors. While your competitors are wasting thousands of dollars on useless newspaper, radio and television ads that are no longer effective, you will be quietly building yourself a loyal following of premium patients. Prospects, who actually care about reputable businesses and well-known owners, are the kind of quality buyers you can build your business on.

Writing a book also has many other side benefits, just like many of the other strategies I've revealed to you. For starters, local media outlets love businesses that publish books and educational materials for the local market. Secondly, you also gain the fame and celebrity status in your marketplace which brings other opportunities because you have done something that most other Dental Practices refuse to invest the time to do.

When it comes down to actually writing your book, you can hire a ghostwriter to write a two hundred page book, or you can spend a few months writing it yourself. A ghostwriter is a writer that you would hire to write a book, but you would have exclusive rights to say that you are the author. In my opinion, you are better off hiring a ghostwriter who knows your industry to write your book, because you can reap the benefits of being a published author in a matter of weeks instead of waiting months or years while you personally write your book. Once your book is written, you can then self-publish it using any number of online services which provide that option.

My consulting firm offers a book writing service with a unique twist. Rather than completely writing a book for a client, we conduct a series of strategic phone interviews that, once professionally transcribed, becomes the book! This is the fastest and easiest way to get your book written. If you would like to discuss this method of getting your book written and published in less than 60 days, just contact my office.

PART FIVE:

Paid Advertising Strategies with Potential for Great Returns on Your Investment

CHAPTER 39

Old Faithful: Profitable Newspaper Advertising

With the invention of the internet, businesses who invest in newspaper advertising has taken a huge nosedive. However, when done correctly, newspaper advertising can be very profitable for businesses. There are still millions of Americans who faithfully read the newspaper and continue to be exposed to ads each and every day of the week. In the advertising age which we live in, your marketing message must be much more appealing to generate the type of buzz that could have been generated ten years ago with the same type of ad.

The caveat with advertising in the newspaper for most businesses is the inability of advertisers to create ads which actually attract the target prospect and compels them to take action. When you are spending thousand dollars per month on advertising in local newspapers, you need to make sure that your target market is not only seeing your ads, but also responding by coming into your business and purchasing.

Writing and creating newspaper ads requires the skill of an experienced marketer and writer. Sadly, if you think that the ad representative from the newspaper, who receives a commission from selling you the advertising space, is the best person to design and create your newspaper marketing campaign, you are in for a long and expensive ride. If you remember nothing else I have written in this book, remember to hire an experienced direct response marketing writer and marketing expert to create ALL of your ads, emails and marketing materials.

The ads you place in your local newspaper should have a headline and content which cause your patient prospects to immediately grab the phone, visit a website or rush into your office and sign-up for your marketing list or purchase your dental services. If you are running ads and you are seeing little to no action from the ads, then you are not creating ads which resonate with your target market. Moreover, you need to make sure every single ad is a direct-response focused approach.

CHAPTER 40

How to Create Profitable
Radio Commercials

When done correctly, radio commercials can have a tremendous profitable impact on your business. However, very similar to newspaper advertising, there is a skill required to create ads and promotional offers which coax prospects to your website to request your educational material or into your business to make buying decisions.

One of the biggest benefits of radio advertising is your ability to select a really targeted group of prospects and focus on attracting them to your business. With radio, you have a chance to make a personal connection with your prospects by using your voice. Prospects will hear your voice and marketing message and can determine for themselves if you sound warm and inviting or cold and forceful like a pushy salesman. If you were one of the one percent of the population who was born with the natural ability to sound like a used car salesman, even if you are not, then you will definitely need to hire the local radio station talent to record your marketing message. Otherwise record your commercials in your own voice.

Writing and recording radio commercials that generate profits is much like creating any other type of marketing campaign. In fact, you should design your radio commercial by using your existing successful ads which you are using in other parts of your business and use those advertising pieces to provide your content for speaking. If you have done your job correctly, your marketing message and USP should be identical.

One of the drawbacks of using radio is the restriction on the length of your advertising space. In most cases you will be dealing with fifteen or thirty seconds spots. Shorter advertising spaces mean that your marketing message will have to be clear and to the point. Additionally, you should absolutely use a different website or phone number to track your incoming calls from each and every radio station you are investing in for your business.

CHAPTER 41

The Secret to Creating Profitable Television Commercials for Your Practice

Advertising on television is the Holy Grail for most small to medium businesses. However, unless a television commercial is scripted and recorded in a certain manner, it will most certainly be a waste of money. Very much like radio advertising, television ads which include the actual owners, staff and actual patients will give prospects a revealing look inside the minds of the owners, and should match the image you want to communicate about your business.

Most small Dental Practices think they do not have budget to advertise on television, therefore, they never even attempt to explore this strategy. Advertising on television has several requirements which will practically guarantee success, if followed carefully. The first requirement to your success is to understand and know your target market. If you haven't taken the time or resources to clearly define your target market, you will needlessly waste tons of money on television advertising.

The second requirement to television advertising is you must work with an ad agency that can negotiate the price of your airtime in bundles with other local businesses. This will allow you to get much better pricing than if you went to a television station directly.

When it comes to actual production of your commercial, if you work with a local television studio, you will be expected to spend anywhere from twenty five hundred dollars to five thousands dollars per thirty second commercial. However, if you really want a huge production with tons of special effects, then expect to spend much more money than that. At the end of the day, you must look at the cost of your television advertising campaign as an investment in your business, which must have a positive return on the money you've invested. Again, as we have covered in previous chapters, you must include a way for the viewers to get more information from your website so that you can automatically follow up with them. This could be a "special TV offer" of a discount or a package of coupons you put together with other local business owners. Follow-up is critical to maximize your investment.

CHAPTER 42

Advertising in Your Local
Coupon Booklet

When it comes to inexpensive marketing ideas with potential for maximum profits, advertising in local coupon booklets is near the top of the list. Coupon booklets have the ability to generate tremendous profits because prospects are already looking through the book because they want a bargain. Therefore, placing your advertisements in the book puts you directly in the path of potential buyers.

When advertising in coupon booklets, testing revealed that the most effective strategy requires that you create an actual coupon for your prospects. Many times when browsing through coupon booklets I see advertisers who have nice little ads, but neglect to include a coupon for patients to bring into their business for an additional discount. When you include a coupon with your advertising you are better able to track your results to know which coupon gave you the best return on your investment. You may also want to consider a special website or webpage just for your coupon book prospects. Having a special website also allows you to know the impact your marketing efforts are having in driving traffic to your website.

Knowing and truly understanding your target market pays huge dividends when it comes to creating an ad for coupon booklets. One of the biggest challenges for businesses, who advertise in coupon booklets, is the lack of physical space on the page. However, this doesn't have to be a thorn in your side, if you know what you target market really desires. In fact, it makes it easier to create ads. With the proper information in your hand, you can create headlines and promotions which specifically motivate your target market to take immediate action. Choose an attention-grabbing heading and a few select bullet points that would appeal to a specific group of patients you work with. This may be teeth whitening for example, where you could offer a free report on how to choose the best dentist for this service. The mere fact that you are offering this resource with the guidance of your answers will position you as a trusted advisor.

Again, as we have covered in previous chapters, you must include a way for them to get more information from your website so that you can automatically follow up with them. When you have this in place, your follow-up happens on autopilot and you generate new patients with ease.

CHAPTER 43

The True Power of Posters, Leaflets and Flyer Inserts

Sometimes the simplest things can lead to extraordinary success. That's the best way to describe the positive effect that a properly prepared marketing campaign which includes posters, leaflets and flyers, can have on your business.

In most neighborhoods and communities there are spaces reserved in highly visible areas, which allow flyers and posters to notify residents of upcoming local events. Usually the areas that towns and neighborhoods reserve for hanging posters and leaflets are also a high-traffic area, so you can really benefit from an effective poster or leaflets.

You can even use posters on the front of your business windows to drive traffic to your website or into your business. However the overall success of your poster, leaflet and flyer campaign will be dependent on your ability to create an irresistible offer. The promotional offer you create for your posters and leaflet campaign must have more than just discounts. You should also consider special packaging or giving away free items in exchange for prospects purchasing specific dollar amounts.

Another powerful way to use flyers and inserts is to contact your local newspapers and have them distributed in the weekly freebie newspapers. This ensures that you reach every household in a specific area and usually the pricing for this service is very reasonable. (don't forget the lead follow-up mechanism so that you can convert the leads into patients!)

CHAPTER 44

Customized Promotions & Sales
For Every Customer

What if you had the power to look into your patients mind and pinpoint the exact products and services they wanted to buy? How much easier would it be to make huge profits in your business? Well, if you have sold to a customer before, then you already have a glimpse into their wants and needs and you probably have never even realized it.

One of the most under-appreciated strategies that I commonly see Dental Practices neglect to implement into their business is the tracking of customer purchases in order to offer additional pieces. See, if a customer has already purchased pieces of a specific product line or collection, then you know that 99% of the time they will be willing to consider adding similar products and services. This is one area of your business which can catapult your business profits.

In order for you to use this strategy, you must write orders or generate computerized receipts which give every detail about your customer's purchase. For example, you will want to know the collection name, the exact products or services they purchased, their size, color and price discounting etc. The best way to use this information is to use a computer program to generate your receipts and track your customer's purchases.

Once you have specific information about a customer's purchase, every couple of months you can create a promotion or ad to generate sales. If they had their teeth whitened, now maybe they need an electric toothbrush!

CHAPTER 45

Maximum Profits with Magazine Advertising

While I'm a huge fan of free publicity marketing strategies, you must have a balanced marketing plan. Advertising in local magazines is not only an effective marketing strategy, but you will be better able to predict your leads, patients and overall return on investment consistently when using paid advertising strategies like this one. This is especially true when you have a proven ad that can bring you consistent results. When you are investing in advertising strategies for magazines, you should only be using an ad that is a proven winner. Advertising space in magazines is usually more expensive than advertising in newspapers, so you need to have a pretty good idea that your promotion is effective and has the ability to get you results before you invest the money in this strategy.

There are some tricks to creating effective magazine ads, but the principles which govern successful advertising still apply. For example, you will need a headline which draws attention from your target market and presents a compelling benefit or reason for the prospect to continue reading the rest of your ad. When you get into investing larger amounts into your advertising, the tracking system that you use becomes even more important, because you will want to instantly know the return on your investment. Keep in mind that your tracking system can be a coupon that the customer has to bring into your business or simply a special website which they can use to purchase the product online.

When advertising in magazines, be prepared to spend a few extra bucks on top-notch design work as well. Magazines tend to be sticklers about the level of professionalism they want to communicate to their readers and subscribers. The perfect situation is for you to have a partnership with a local designer, who will create all of your ads for you.

If you have a local magazine that is dedicated to your local area you will have a much better impact. This is because they already are used to frequenting local businesses. You can also combine this with the publicity strategy of writing short educational articles for the magazine. Remember to mention your website, charity events, internet TV shows etc.

PART EIGHT:

BONUS: High-Powered Advanced Marketing Strategies

CHAPTER 46

Be a Radio Show Guest
On Local Stations

An effective strategy which attracts patients by the carloads is to become a local celebrity. One of the fastest ways to become well known in a marketplace is to be everywhere your target market hangs out or shops. One of the ways to build your celebrity status is to become a regular guest on the local radio circuit. Very few Dental Practices have ever considered being a radio guest as a way to connect with their prospects and patients while growing their business.

The reason why being a radio show guest is so effective is because radio show hosts have already taken the time to build relationships with their listeners and you can piggy back off of their success. The truth of the matter is that every radio station needs guests to fill their airtime for their audience.

The first step in this process is to figure out the radio programs that your prospects listen to on a regular basis. You can accomplish this by asking your patients and prospects on a survey form on your website or in your business. You can reward them for providing the information by giving them a coupon for a discount.

Once you have that information, you should begin to listen to those specific radio stations for at least a week or more. Listening to the station will provide you with the general flow and outline of the best programming on that station. After you get a good feel for a station, you can then begin to come up with an interesting angle or story hook to get their attention.

When you have your story angle or hook, you can then hire a writer to write a press release around your idea. You can hire a pretty good writer from websites like Cragislist.com or Getafreelancer.com. The writer should also be able to send your press releases to your target radio shows at least once or twice each month for a monthly retainer fee. Your press release will also give the radio station your contact information and story idea. If the radio station chooses your story idea they will contact you for more information on your story idea. Of course, your ultimate goal is to be invited to be a guest for one of their shows.

Being a radio show guest does require some skills which you will have to develop in order to be a good guest. For example, you must be entertaining, educational and quick on your feet. It's very much like working with a customer in your office or business, except that you will be speaking into microphone. There are several programs online which instruct you on how to be a radio show guest, so you may want to invest in one of those programs before implementing this strategy into your business.

Again, as we have covered in previous chapters, you must include a way for the listeners to get more information from your website so that you can automatically follow up with them.

CHAPTER 47

Guest Blogger on Local
Blogs & Websites

Being a guest blogger on other local blogs and websites is one of the more advanced and effective online strategies. This is one step away from being a true joint venture strategy, but it is equally as effective when done properly. In fairness, this strategy does require that you be a decent writer and have the ability to "write on demand". If your writing skills are not up to par, you can always hire a writer to write short articles for you and then post those articles on other blogs.

The huge benefit of this strategy is your implied positioning as the go-to expert to your target market, simply because you are the author of a informative and educational blog posting. However, in order to accomplish this goal, you must partner with blogs and websites which cater to your target market.

The best way to discover who your target market, is to review your previous customer receipts and compile the information into a spreadsheet. Once you have the information into an easily understandable format, you can then analyze the data to see specific patterns and trends.

Your next step is to find patients, friends or family members who match the same target demographic as your past patients. Ask them for recommendations of websites and blogs which they frequently visit. You may get lucky and be able to be a featured guest blogger on one of the websites they mention or you may have to find similar websites in your local target market. In either case, your business will greatly benefit from you being viewed as a source of credible information about your products and services.

Once you find websites or blogs that match your target market, there are several ways to contact the blog authors and owners. The first method is a little more stealthy, but basically you just post comments on their blog for a couple of weeks and then email them to let them know that you have written a couple of articles which would make a very good blog posting for a specific niche. It's important that you don't come across as a salesperson for your business or a specific product, but as a author you is willing to provide some informative blog postings for their blog audience.

The second way to contact blog authors and owners is to email them and ask directly if you could be a guest blogger. You will have to email them a copy of your articles that you have written or have paid to have written for you. Once they see that you are serious about giving them good information to post on their blogs, you will definitely have a better chance of becoming a regular guest blogger.

CHAPTER 48

Start Your Own Blog

Most Dental Practices are content to simply have a nice website, but super-successful small to medium businesses know that they may need something more for their online strategies to be successful. That's why having a blog becomes more of a necessity.

A blog is a website that allows you to add text, video or pictures instantly without needing to know computer coding or hiring tech guys to reprogram your website. Websites like Wordpress.com and Blogger.com will give you a free blog and will walk you through the setup process. This is not recommended because the free option does not allow for the critical plugins needed to make your blog posts and pages easily found by the search engines like Google. It is very easy to set up your own hosted blog for about $5 per month, the service I recommend is www.SmallBusinessBlogHosting.com. Then having a skilled Wordpress consultant strategically set up your blog can allow you to rank on Google page #1 in a matter of weeks! This is a great way to get high Google rankings rather than to attempt to work on an existing site you have with poor rankings.

One of the great features of having a blog is your ability to post content online, therefore communicating with your target market without expensive advertising or marketing costs. Blogs also have a feature which allows your visitors to post comments and text, videos or pictures of their own. This allows you to build a relationship of communication with your target prospects. Of course, this comes with some risk. If you have a prospect or customer who is not happy with your company, product or service, then your blog may serve as a most convenient place for them to voice all of their disapproval…but you will set the blog up so that you have to approve each comment before it is live.

However, the best benefit of having a blog is the ability to plug into other popular "social media" websites which are heavily visited by internet users in every target market in the world. Social media websites are websites where the visitors and users have the ability to interact with each other and create online groups or communities of individuals of similar interests.

The success of most strategies such as this one, hinge on your ability to know your target market and create content, products and services which will entice your ideal customer to visit your blog and ultimately, choose your business for their product or service.

CHAPTER 49

Start Your Own Internet Radio Show

Admittedly, this is an advanced strategy, but if you have the willingness to learn new things, then you can implement this strategy into your business and make huge profits from the fame. While advertising on the radio can be profitable, it can become extremely expensive if you try to increase your marketing campaign too quickly. There is a way to avoid those costs altogether, and become famous too. For the smart business owner, the future of free publicity strategies is internet radio shows. This may come as a total shock to you, but there are internet radio websites which allow you to start your own internet radio show for free. Websites like Blogtalkradio.com and Shoutcast.com allow anyone who has a computer and microphone to create their own radio show. This means you can become an overnight star if you have the talent and ability to put together a program and event on a fairly consistent basis.

The benefit of starting your own internet radio show is that you do not have to pay for radio air-time and you can create and air a show as often as you like. You also benefit because you are the one calling the shots and writing the content for your show. This means that you can make it as commercial as you desire, unlike some of the free publicity strategies.

When creating your own radio show, you can schedule the programming to be as long or as short as you see fit. For example, you can create a one hour show which airs once per week or more. You can also script the show to include guest speakers or just simply be built around your business. However, it is in your best interest to create a show that is informative and entertaining because prospects always trying to escape everyday life. If your show can provide that entertainment, then your show will practically be guaranteed to succeed.

The real worth of this strategy is in your ability to get an audience filled with your target market. One of the best ways to do this is by posting a link to your radio show on your own website and on the website of your joint venture partners. You can also post your radio show ad on various other online websites where your target market hangs out.

CHAPTER 50

Marketing Your Business with Online Videos

Video marketing is one of the most effective online marketing strategies, but it's also one of the most advanced strategies for small to medium Dental Practices. The real power of video marketing is its ability to connect your audience to you emotionally and visually. When done correctly, video marketing can reach thousands of prospects in your target market for little to no money out of pocket.

The video marketing campaign strategy involves recording one to three minute videos describing the benefits of your products or services online to hundreds of prospects everyday, without actually leaving your business. You can even use a short video to introduce a specific collection and then have the patients view the remainder of the information from your basic website. The best part about video marketing is that you can post your video on popular websites like Youtube.com and begin funneling Youtube.com visitors back to your own website.

While video marketing will require you to have some basic knowledge of camera's and computer software, the benefits far outweigh the learning curve. In fact, you can spend as little as two or three hours getting familiar with the equipment and then begin profiting from this strategy. In my opinion, the best type of video recorder for newbie's is the flip video recorder, which costs less than one hundred dollars, and shoots pretty decent footage. You can then record yourself presenting a specific product and give your prospects a live tour of your office and staff. Using video to describe your products and services allows your patients to build a personal relationship with you.

If you do not want to learn how to do all of that, my firm has a service that will create professional video commercials and distribute and syndicate them online. When done properly, this can allow you to have your website appear on Google page #1 along with a video and a Press Release.

When your potential patients Google your local town + dentists and they see you, with multiple positions, your credibility shoots through the roof.

If you would like help with this just contact our office.

CHAPTER 51

Social Media

No matter what you may think about social media, it is a powerful force in today's business world. There is literally no way to explore all of the benefits your Dental Practice can enjoy from integrating social media into your practice in this chapter. But consider this: what if every time you wrote an article and posted it on your blog, it also was automatically posted to your Facebook page, Twitter account, Linkedin account and sent to your email list? This saves so much time in logging into each service to post and update. The power of doing this is that when your patients follow you on social media, their friends also see your information show up in their newsfeed! When you appear on a radio show or do a video they see this because it is posted through your social media accounts. The power of social proof is huge and needs to be harnessed in your Dental Practice.

I wrote a book on Social Media Marketing which I highly recommend you buy and read...not just because I wrote it, but because it is a fun book to read. It integrates an MBA level marketing strategy into social media and is told in story-format. You can go to Amazon and search for "The P.R.I.S.M. Salvation" or visit www.ThePrismSalvation.com

About The Author

Mike Saunders holds an MBA in Marketing and serves the small and medium-sized business market and can help your Dental Practice dramatically increase leads, prospects and profits while minimizing your marketing expenses.

In addition to coaching and consulting clients in his firm Marketing Huddle LLC, Teaching Marketing as an Adjunct Marketing Professor at select Colleges and Universities, Mike also is a Marketing Consultant with the Denver Small Business Development Center (SBDC).

His unique application of Marketing Integration Principles helps his clients use the Internet to grow their businesses quickly while reducing marketing and advertising costs.

By visiting www.MarketingHuddle.com you can get a Free chapter of his books on social media and goal setting, published on Amazon.

His perspective is unique because while he consults with Dental Practices, he also works with a variety of small businesses and therefore has insights, strategies and very effective business-building techniques that are significantly different than the average consultant.

Mike has been married for 15 years and has three daughters and a son. He enjoys spending time at his family's cabin in the mountains of Colorado, hiking and riding ATVs, and enjoys playing acoustic guitar in the College and Career Sunday School class he teaches at church.

www.MarketingHuddle.com

"Claim Your <u>FREE</u> Marketing Audit That Uncovers Marketing Assets Currently Within Your Dental Practice That Are Not Being Maximized And Easily Increase Your Sales By 25% - 50% In 90 Days or Less Without Spending More Money On Advertising!"
($497 Value)

Details revealed below...

Mike Saunders, MBA author and dynamic marketing consultant, is offering an <u>**FREE**</u> incredible opportunity for you to improve your current marketing and sales systems without spending more money on advertising. Claim your free marketing audit today and discover:

- How to **quickly increase your sales by 25% - 50% in the next 90 days** without spending more money on advertising!

- How to **guarantee that your business stands head and shoulders above the competition**, so prospects will be proud and excited to buy from you.

- The **"Hidden Goldmine"** in your business and how you can capitalize on it and make big profits.

Claim Your FREE Marketing Audit and read our Dental Social Media Case Study...

www.DentalMarketingFusion.com